This Book Be

_____

_____

_____

_____

_____

_____

EMERGENCY CONTACT

Name: _____

Relationship: _____

Address: _____

_____

Contact Number: _____

Email Address: _____

NOTES

_____

_____

_____

_____

_____

Signature Planner Journals

www.signatureplannerjournals.com
www.signatureplannerjournals.co.uk

TRAVEL ITINERARY

DAY	ACTIVITY/ EVENT

 # TRAVEL ITINERARY

DAY	ACTIVITY/ EVENT

THINGS TO BRING

ELECTRONICS	QTY	OTHER	QTY
☐ Cell Phone		☐	
☐ Charger		☐	
☐ Tablet		☐	
☐ Camera		☐	
☐ iPod/ MP3 Player		☐	
☐ Batteries		☐	
☐		☐	
☐		☐	
☐		☐	
☐		☐	

Day	
	Date _____
	Destination _____
	With Who? _____

Today we went to...

I saw...

I ate...

I heard...

I touched...

I learned...

My Favorite thing was...

I am thankful...

Day	Date
	Destination
	With Who?

Today we went to...

I saw...

I ate...

I heard...

I touched...

I learned...

My Favorite thing was...

I am thankful...

Day	Date
	Destination
	With Who?

Today we went to...

I saw...

I ate...

I heard...

I touched...

I learned...

My Favorite thing was...

I am thankful...

Day	Date _____
	Destination _____
	With Who? _____

Today we went to...

I saw...

I ate...

I heard...

I touched...

I learned...

My Favorite thing was...

I am thankful...

Day	Date
	Destination
	With Who?

Today we went to...

I saw...

I ate...

I heard...

I touched...

I learned...

My Favorite thing was...

I am thankful...

Day	Date
	Destination
	With Who?

Today we went to...

I saw...

I ate...

I heard...

I touched...

I learned...

My Favorite thing was...

I am thankful...

Day	Date
	Destination
	With Who?

Today we went to...

I saw...

I ate...

I heard...

I touched...

I learned...

My Favorite thing was...

I am thankful...

Day	Date
	Destination
	With Who?

Today we went to...

I saw...

I ate...

I heard...

I touched...

I learned...

My Favorite thing was...

I am thankful...

Day	Date
	Destination
	With Who?

Today we went to...

I saw...

I ate...

I heard...

I touched...

I learned...

My Favorite thing was...

I am thankful...

Day	Date _____
	Destination _____
	With Who? _____

Today we went to...

I saw...

I ate...

I heard...

I touched...

I learned...

My Favorite thing was...

I am thankful...

Day	Date
	Destination
	With Who?

Today we went to...

I saw...

I ate...

I heard...

I touched...

I learned...

My Favorite thing was...

I am thankful...

Day	Date
	Destination
	With Who?

Today we went to...

I saw...

I ate...

I heard...

I touched...

I learned...

My Favorite thing was...

I am thankful...

Day	Date
	Destination
	With Who?

Today we went to...

I saw...

I ate...

I heard...

I touched...

I learned...

My Favorite thing was...

I am thankful...

Day	Date
	Destination
	With Who?

Today we went to...

I saw...

I ate...

I heard...

I touched...

I learned...

My Favorite thing was...

I am thankful...

Day	Date
	Destination
	With Who?

Today we went to...

I saw...

I ate...

I heard...

I touched...

I learned...

My Favorite thing was...

I am thankful...

Day	Date
	Destination
	With Who?

Today we went to...

I saw...

I ate...

I heard...

I touched...

I learned...

My Favorite thing was...

I am thankful...

Day	Date
	Destination
	With Who?

Today we went to...

I saw...

I ate...

I heard...

I touched...

I learned...

My Favorite thing was...

I am thankful...

Day	Date
	Destination
	With Who?

Today we went to...

I saw...

I ate...

I heard...

I touched...

I learned...

My Favorite thing was...

I am thankful...

Day	Date
	Destination
	With Who?

Today we went to...

I saw...

I ate...

I heard...

I touched...

I learned...

My Favorite thing was...

I am thankful...

Day	Date
	Destination
	With Who?

Today we went to...

I saw...

I ate...

I heard...

I touched...

I learned...

My Favorite thing was...

I am thankful...

Day	Date
	Destination
	With Who?

Today we went to...

I saw...

I ate...

I heard...

I touched...

I learned...

My Favorite thing was...

I am thankful...

Day	Date _____
	Destination _____
	With Who? _____

Today we went to...

I saw...

I ate...

I heard...

I touched...

I learned...

My Favorite thing was...

I am thankful...

Day	Date
	Destination
	With Who?

Today we went to...

I saw...

I ate...

I heard...

I touched...

I learned...

My Favorite thing was...

I am thankful...

Day	Date
	Destination
	With Who?

Today we went to...

I saw...

I ate...

I heard...

I touched...

I learned...

My Favorite thing was...

I am thankful...

Day	Date _____
	Destination _____
	With Who? _____

Today we went to...

I saw...

I ate...

I heard...

I touched...

I learned...

My Favorite thing was...

I am thankful...

Day	Date
	Destination
	With Who?

Today we went to...

I saw...

I ate...

I heard...

I touched...

I learned...

My Favorite thing was...

I am thankful...

Day	Date
	Destination
	With Who?

Today we went to...

I saw...

I ate...

I heard...

I touched...

I learned...

My Favorite thing was...

I am thankful...

Day	Date
	Destination
	With Who?

Today we went to...

I saw...

I ate...

I heard...

I touched...

I learned...

My Favorite thing was...

I am thankful...

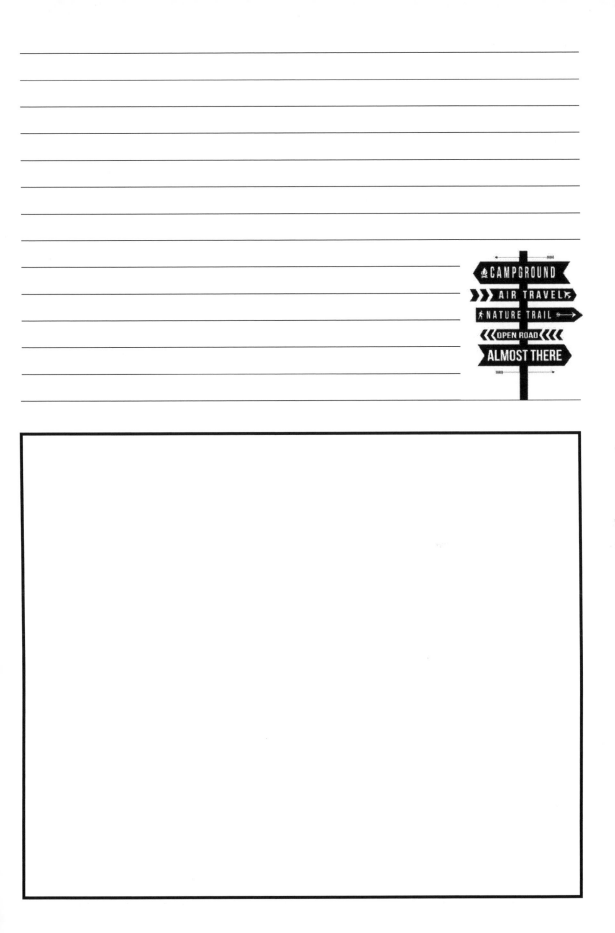

Day	Date
	Destination
	With Who?

Today we went to...

I saw...

I ate...

I heard...

I touched...

I learned...

My Favorite thing was...

I am thankful...

Day	Date
	Destination
	With Who?

Today we went to...

I saw...

I ate...

I heard...

I touched...

I learned...

My Favorite thing was...

I am thankful...

Day	Date
	Destination
	With Who?

Today we went to...

I saw...

I ate...

I heard...

I touched...

I learned...

My Favorite thing was...

I am thankful...

Day	Date
	Destination
	With Who?

Today we went to...

I saw...

I ate...

I heard...

I touched...

I learned...

My Favorite thing was...

I am thankful...

Day	Date
	Destination
	With Who?

Today we went to...

I saw...

I ate...

I heard...

I touched...

I learned...

My Favorite thing was...

I am thankful...

Day	Date
	Destination
	With Who?

Today we went to...

I saw...

I ate...

I heard...

I touched...

I learned...

My Favorite thing was...

I am thankful...

Day	Date
	Destination
	With Who?

Today we went to...

I saw...

I ate...

I heard...

I touched...

I learned...

My Favorite thing was...

I am thankful...

Day	Date
	Destination
	With Who?

Today we went to...

I saw...

I ate...

I heard...

I touched...

I learned...

My Favorite thing was...

I am thankful...

Day	Date
	Destination
	With Who?

Today we went to...

I saw...

I ate...

I heard...

I touched...

I learned...

My Favorite thing was...

I am thankful...

Day	Date
	Destination
	With Who?

Today we went to...

I saw...

I ate...

I heard...

I touched...

I learned...

My Favorite thing was...

I am thankful...

Day	Date
	Destination
	With Who?

Today we went to...

I saw...

I ate...

I heard...

I touched...

I learned...

My Favorite thing was...

I am thankful...

Day	Date _____
	Destination _____
	With Who? _____

Today we went to...

I saw...

I ate...

I heard...

I touched...

I learned...

My Favorite thing was...

I am thankful...

Day	Date _____
	Destination _____
	With Who? _____

Today we went to...

I saw...

I ate...

I heard...

I touched...

I learned...

My Favorite thing was...

I am thankful...

Day	Date _____
	Destination _____
	With Who? _____

Today we went to...

I saw...

I ate...

I heard...

I touched...

I learned...

My Favorite thing was...

I am thankful...

Day	Date
	Destination
	With Who?

Today we went to...

I saw...

I ate...

I heard...

I touched...

I learned...

My Favorite thing was...

I am thankful...

Day	Date _____
	Destination _____
	With Who? _____

Today we went to...

I saw...

I ate...

I heard...

I touched...

I learned...

My Favorite thing was...

I am thankful...

Day	Date
	Destination
	With Who?

Today we went to...

I saw...

I ate...

I heard...

I touched...

I learned...

My Favorite thing was...

I am thankful...

Day	Date
	Destination
	With Who?

Today we went to...

I saw...

I ate...

I heard...

I touched...

I learned...

My Favorite thing was...

I am thankful...

Day	Date
	Destination
	With Who?

Today we went to...

I saw...

I ate...

I heard...

I touched...

I learned...

My Favorite thing was...

I am thankful...

Day	Date
	Destination
	With Who?

Today we went to...

I saw...

I ate...

I heard...

I touched...

I learned...

My Favorite thing was...

I am thankful...

Day	Date
	Destination
	With Who?

Today we went to...

I saw...

I ate...

I heard...

I touched...

I learned...

My Favorite thing was...

I am thankful...

Day	Date
	Destination
	With Who?

Today we went to...

I saw...

I ate...

I heard...

I touched...

I learned...

My Favorite thing was...

I am thankful...

Day	Date
	Destination
	With Who?

Today we went to...

I saw...

I ate...

I heard...

I touched...

I learned...

My Favorite thing was...

I am thankful...

Day	Date
	Destination
	With Who?

Today we went to...

I saw...

I ate...

I heard...

I touched...

I learned...

My Favorite thing was...

I am thankful...

Day	Date
	Destination
	With Who?

Today we went to...

I saw...

I ate...

I heard...

I touched...

I learned...

My Favorite thing was...

I am thankful...

Day	Date
	Destination
	With Who?

Today we went to...

I saw...

I ate...

I heard...

I touched...

I learned...

My Favorite thing was...

I am thankful...

Day	Date
	Destination
	With Who?

Today we went to...

I saw...

I ate...

I heard...

I touched...

I learned...

My Favorite thing was...

I am thankful...

Made in the USA
Monee, IL
05 July 2022

99108264R00066

Made in the USA
Monee, IL
05 July 2022